AF327006

PRESENTS

Judyl Mudfoot

Mudborn Press   1977   Santa Barbara

Copyright © 1977 Judyl Mudfoot

"for Jack and Dorothy" and "no more presents" appeared in *Rockbottom* 2 (Fall 1976); "for Elizabeth" in *The Santa Barbara News & Review* (July 18, 1975); "for Sasha" in *Womanfire* (September 1975)

Photo by Sasha Newborn

Printed in USA

ISBN 0-930012-02-x (paper)
ISBN 0-930012-03-8 (cloth)

Mudborn Press, 209 W. De la Guerra, Santa Barbara 93101

These poems are what I have—what I found to say but also what's left: what's moved into words and stays fixed on the page.

I'd like to remember I've always made presents (I wanted to). That on May Day, 1949, every doorstep in my neighborhood had a beautiful basket full of fresh woodsflowers for the people inside. That when I cared, I did something, made something at least as well as I could.

I tried paint, clay, wool, finally words. Until I spoke to someone who mattered, I had no voice. That's how I've been able to work. Two of the people and the one other creature named in my titles are dead; four are years away; we've all changed. The work is what's left.

Judyl

they've been together
now 3 years
since her stroke
she rarely goes out
never alone
and can't talk much
pushed back before speech
old for another beginning
but she smiles
with an almost memory
and much kindness
positions my legs
and arms so I
stand (awkwardly)
as she was—a ballerina
and calls me beautiful

in her eyes
when confusion
clears for a moment
when she can be
not alone
I see beauty that's
not in the past
she moves slowly

becomes young
as she is
delicate hands
emptying ashtrays
goodness not blocked
by impairment
she cares for her house
and for us
lights her own
cigarette

and she knows
when to say loudly
Stop it!
No no no no
No way!
when we've lost
all she still has
when we get trapped
in harsh words
lose ourselves
in our roles
in our speeches
cut the small
threads between us
with irrelevant
violent gestures

her children won't
visit her drunk,
sick, down and out
and not married

though he keeps the house
clean and cheerful
hides the old bottles
in plain brown sacks
in the garbage

disoriented by
cheap strong wine and
hopeless repetition
I listen, wanting
again the clear
voice from the sky
telling us, You're
all right, everyone's
all right

he tells her, I love you
you old bitch, and
means it
he cooks me a
whole greasy fish
with mushrooms
because I'm hungry

I've had a dozen
perhaps children, held each
a day or 2, felt full
I went thru it all once, right
on your floor—you didn't believe me
thought I'd been there before,
given birth to a dead one
or a monster or at least
had a painful abortion—
afterwards there was no one,
nothing who hadn't been
with us before, but my dreams
are as real and as empty
as any recollection

and the blondyoung kid
who climbed down inside me
in the 6-person railway
compartment somewhere between
Florence and Naples didn't
believe I was virgin
but we were children
together anyway for
3 days in a drab hotel

he played a wood flute
as we climbed up
thru the terraced almonds
in bloom and I met
an old woman in black
who gave me her wisdom

your mother told me
of the birth
of each
of her 3 sons
as a present

I've traveled and listened—
next time we're out late
let me introduce you
to the large Abyssinian cat
who waits for me
at the corner
I'll take all my charms,
tie garlic by its roots
to my beads so not all
of my phantoms can find us

I know that
the small tree
that grows in my hedge
is a loquat because
a neighbor told me—
it's borne no fruit

the wind
makes a different sound
thru the drying palmbranch
beginning to let go
and thru the bright green
newly tasseled corn

the wind bores into my head
thru my ears
dogs bark and this car
keeps turning in front of me
cutting me off, slicing
my pumpkingold path with its
black spinning rubbered wheels
so I can't find
where it is I'm going

stale energy clogging my pores
so I can't wash
myself clean with fresh sweat
comfort my small lonely breasts
in salt-water pools of their own

my hair droops and I'm frowsy
so I can't sulk
without feeling self-conscious
can't remember to go
here and there as if
nothing had happened
can't curl my arms tight
round my body and sleep

knowing the lost path
might wind back
to the last turn
where I relaxed into
wide open electrification
in 31 delicious colors
as gentleness touched my arm
smiled into my smile

wanting the dream between my legs
aches me alive again
week-old kitten
in the middle of the pile
with a teat in my mouth
laughter of children
dancing a ring in the sky

knowing magic's still here
if I reach out
in any direction
and there's no
reason at all
why it can't
be that simple

you called your dream
"revolution," called me
"beauty," but my way
of choosing a life
was finding a man
and you weren't
what I wanted

you stank of the
cheap fortified wine
you used against the pain
of each human maimed,
dead, or imprisoned
you stumbled and broke things
when you reached out
with your poems, with
songs in French, songs
from underground Spain
you'd almost destroyed yourself
with your love for us all

I couldn't speak, couldn't help,
couldn't bury myself in your
dark room, add myself to the
piles of books and old clothes,
sacks of crumpled paper
and empty bottles

a nice Jewish boy
came down from the Bronx
on weekends—late Friday
nights I scrubbed my
fiberboard floors, scrubbed myself,
slept a few hours on a
bare foam mattress (ironed sheets
still in the laundry package)
got up early to haul
the best food on 1st Ave.
up 4 flights of stairs

I didn't want your dirt
(or mine) on his cock, I
wouldn't be a carrier
of chaos and clap

I came to find out
you were still alive,
to tell you goodbye
and saw you in a photo
on the wall—a young boy
in a starched middy
with a different name—
found out you had parents

you had to cry before
I'd jack you off, had to
show me where
to put my thumb

touch is only a small
link between people
who need and dream

I lived securely,
ate compromise til I
recognized the taste
and gagged, broke the rules,
left hardwood lemon-oiled floors
and found what I thought was
a mystic who paid his rent
washed himself and his dishes,
cleaned out the catbox;
found my name and built
my dream in the space
he cleared for me:
it was retroactively smashed
when he told me he'd never felt
that I was his twin
that he'd let me find my own way
because he felt helpless;
when I knew we'd shared only
our words and the feel of our bodies

now I need a few beers
to reach out
to kiss strangers

some mornings
coffee and cigarettes
aren't enough
don't stop my crying
I feel the soft clench
of my own vagina,
give myself fresh come
to smell on my finger
and try to go on

is it our fault?
are we too weak
to dream alive the world?

have you found
what you wanted?

Mrs. Schiavelli,
where are you? I was
counting on you to help us
put it all together after
we spontaneously uprose,
sent people (not delegates)
to our assembly—anyone
to whom 10 neighbors said,
You know me, speak for me

after we shut down the world
long enough to remember
who we are and what we want
we'd seek you out—
you kept 3 generations
fed, clothed and coherent
under 1 roof—what else
did we need, who else
could lead our city?

there'd be no work except
what fed our bodies,
brought us joy—the only
traffic on the expressway
an occasional bus or truck
taking us out to plant or
harvest the divider strips

the plan wasn't worked out
I'd start constructing
it in words for friends
and my dream dissolved
in their laughter

my roots went down
thru the old mattress,
the floor, quickly
past the oil burner, thru
concrete at the bottom
of the basement into
the rock earth of the
island, drawing strength

I pulled them up,
started slowly across the
country wondering when
would someone appear
to enlist me
in the revolution
saying, This is how
we will do it; will
you help us?

when I settled on the
far coast I envied
other people's kitchen
cupboards, started
saying, If I can't do
anything important
at least I want a
dining-room table

I got the table but I
haven't made its room
a world like the warm
space in your house you
reached thru, touching
my shoulder, asking
would I like a
little more to eat

my dreams are lonely
now and I can't give
you power you haven't
thought of and don't want

if I can find
your house again
I won't come hauling
a bannered platform,
clutching plans—I've got
only an empty, open, timid
outstretched hand, a few
words and a little hope

where are you,
Mrs. Schiavelli?

the ring that
binds me together
slipped off as I
gathered stones
to guard the grave
of a kitten
to keep her safe
til she'd left
her fur and bones

now thin black dogs
whose feelings don't
show on their faces
wait to rip me open
at the navel, wait
to snatch and run
trailing my intestines
thru quiet streets

I've slept soundly
with no walls
the great window flung
open to moonlight
on wrecked buildings
and scattered bricks
in the bushes
as the land slopes
to the forest

I remember the clear
white of fresh snow
as I walked home
across lower Manhattan—
tired from a night's
work, tired of waiting
for a last bus that
might not exist—
crisp and alive

I'd put bars on
my windows the
heaviest I could
pay for and carry:
the patterns they made
on my ceiling brought
sleep as the wind moved
tree shadows across them

another night
climbing the stairs
I found blood on
the wall just beyond
the first landing

I remember
laughter

I've thought gently
of you these 20 years
the dignity you kept,
clear eyes the others
couldn't laugh down
when they snatched a
folded note or poem
the turquoise ink
unmistakeable

I never wrote back
but you'd follow me,
wait til I reached
the head of the line
and bow slightly as
you turned the
drinking fountain knob

I was never sure
how a princess acts
and you'd be gone when
I lifted my head
but you'd appear with
a key every time
my skate fell off—
I don't think
we ever spoke

but you found my
grandmother's house
on Christmas Day and
rang the bell and ran—
inside the package
slimy odd-smelling
phosphoresence in
a dark blue bottle
with a card I
quickly hid
because it said
you loved me in
clear round script
above your name

that year my
mother gave me
awkward explanations
and a box of Kotex
that sat unopened
in my drawer when
we moved to
another town

I still deny
nobility, wear
dirty boots but
love and try
to give proudly
against laughter
remembering your gifts

I don't know how
my brain got
damaged—thoughts
come slowly now
with pauses
longer
than the words

I meant to build
you a nest
the color of dawn

we've had too
many words
too little love
too few
places to rest
without sleeping

what if the shadow
of a butterfly
falls
across our breath? the
elders must not
close their ears
against the young

are you and I
the only ones
who have smashed glass
against the wall?
who see new wood
a platform ready
for the dance?

tho' we're both
injured, you walk
tonight without
your cane; I put
the food away
pour wine
I stomp my
foot against the
kitchen floor and
start to sing:
an old song
against the light
against intelligence
drawn thinly out

I've got a
monologue
now no one
listens:
I was born
thin, redfaced
bald and wanting
life—I
haven't changed

would there be
laughter if we
knew
where to go?

I used to know
how to fly—first find
something raised but
solid—an old desk or
an empty pedestal—this
is the platform: once
you get up there, you've
got to begin

crouch low, feet together
knees apart, arms
fully extended

now pause, breathe
deep and know
you've got wings

move them slowly at
first, test the air,
then faster and start
flapping your knees
(if you flap harder
and forget who you are
you won't fall over)

raise and lower your
body (keep flapping!) til
you've got to let it
all go in the air

I always awoke
slightly bruised and
changed after landing

I also did "The Countess"
but I needed 12
feet unobstructed
to run and make my body
completely disjointed
and noble, to end with a
stomped triumphant curtsey

you've seen my
current act—I stand
in the light, solid
under the fuzzy
halo of my hair,
reading words

if I tell you that
who I am has left
me a heifer in the
center of this ring
that all 4 of my feet
have just been neatly
roped, that my nose
hits the ground and

dust blurs the
outlines of my spots:
if I bleat and
struggle will you
see my rope, see me
break it only again
to be suddenly tied?

for Rose

Look, I've got a
brand new wheelbarrow!
it's not a toy: dark green
has always been the color
of my dreams; it will
make me a farmer, a
communard
              you watched
me turn away, saw no one
share my work, my hunger,
left a note: You're
just not
driving it right

                  it's easier
to love a wheelbarrow, a
paintbox I kissed goodnight
instead of my mother—things
stay where I put them, don't
cry
      louder and louder
alone upstairs, awake with
pain in my ankle

no one came so I
limped down and cried
by their beds til my father
gave me liniment
                    I must
have been 14, my room
still pink and taffeta,
not mine—green paint
never gave me a home
in my parents' house
green paint on the truck
hasn't made me a gypsy
or a mechanic
                    knowing
won't bring you back
to my door on your way
to the beach—I was always
working; it's easier
to work than to love you
young and beautiful
                    a child
I was blonde as you, I laughed
as we laughed drinking
Cokes together
on the swings

                    in my house
when no one gave you a ride
out of town, your face red
from the cold, I stopped
working and listened,

gave you my room but
cried when you chose
against my dream, didn't have
the poem you asked for
                         it's
easier to turn away than admit
I have no daughter
I had a Christmas
there's a photo: we're
laughing, you're wearing
the nightgown I made you

if I promise not
to paint you green, will you
sing for me again that
sad song, the one
about your friends?

I came here in
borrowed clothes,
with tidy hair so
you would know me
as your daughter

you haven't spoken
but your eyes
are clear and
seem to focus
on my face

our arms crawl
toward each other
from our sleeves

I see a
large man in a
small bed whose
hand grasps mine
turning white
surprised at
your strength—I'm
trying not to
turn away

only one could
be with you——her voice
shook, kept clarity
but didn't choke
her feeling: "Eskrege,
it's your mother"
I stood aside
read "Mom"
on your dry lips
heard a whisper

I've been proud
to think her blood was
mine from you——is
there a needle
matching yours
inside the elbow of
my other arm? what
shall I do
before I die?

for Blanche

we've come back
from the hospital
it was only
a visit—your
house is a
safe place the
sheets are clean—why
do I dream
these insects?
why do they move
brown, black,
brown-black silent
on the walls and
thru my skull?
I don't
smell anyone
but they're all
here, every variety
of roach and spider
some ants, a few
grey lice but
not a single bee
or dragonfly, no green
no golden, no wingsound

shall I
borrow a bottle
of patent medicine
from a friend and
wake up?

out back with cut grass
drying in scattered
mats hiding new
growth, I admire
a single
unkillable geranium

I keep washing
my hands, clutch
earth with my toes

you kept that
other dream off me,
braced against
wreckage you
couldn't see—it was
cold, sharp and
heavy; it would've
crushed your child

did you know it
came back disguised,
bright-ugly unrecognizable
shapes and loud noises? do
you know a wreck
follows me
down a road
driving, and waits?

you complain only
about ants and
that grasshopper
on your livingroom
wall; that's a
good sign—I heard
it flutter, pale green
into the glass,
antennae alert
may it feed well
in your yard, may
it sing

already I feel
a chill wind
from the canyon, clear
air from the white
ridge reaching
between buildings

when my hair turns
white will I
turn young again
squall and regain
the use
of my other hand,
sit strapped in
at table, surprised,
yelling, I can't
get out of this chair?

I keep expecting
an answer in the mail
read thru fine print and
numbers on the gas bill
check the label on each
advertisement, looking
for my name——if no one
asks or gives, I
disappear, I've no more
presents, no questions

except, What's wrong
with my pencil
my hand, my words false
on the page? I
meant that a
moment ago I
meant something

all night in the
bus station, reading
the same poems over
again I keep myself
awake, keep up
an old shield
out of habit

I watch us all
dying, all waiting
for someone else

Please
stop, don't smile
and walk by, please
eat half this food
so I won't go hungry

help me see how the leaf
curls, how the fruit
grows from the bud,
how to flower and wilt,
to make petals that
won't last forever

Somebody, teach me
how to stop
praying

500 copies letterpressed
from handset Bembo

26 copies signed & lettered,
each with a holograph poem,
handbound in boards